This Notebook Belongs To :

Made in United States
Orlando, FL
24 July 2025

63227628R00069